NICHOLAS YINGLING

THE FIRE ROAD

Cover Design: Catherine Charbonneau
Cover Art: Kevin Cooley
Interior Design: Catherine Charbonneau

Published 2024 by Barrow Street, Inc.
(501) (c) (3) corporation. All contributions are tax deductible.
Distributed by:
  Barrow Street Books
  URI English Department, Swan 114
  60 Upper College Road
  Kingston, RI 02881

Barrow Street Books are also distributed by Small Press
Distribution, SPD, 2625 Alcatraz Ave, #514, Berkeley,
CA 94705-2702, spd@spdbooks.org; (510) 524-1668, (800) 869-7553
(Toll-free within the US); amazon.com; Ingram Periodicals Inc., 1240
Heil Quaker Blvd, PO Box 7000, La Vergne, TN 37086-700 (615)
213-3574; and Armadillo & Co., 7310 S. La Cienega Blvd, Inglewood,
CA 90302, (310) 693-6061.

Special thanks to the University of Rhode Island English Department
and especially the PhD Program in English, 60 Upper College Road,
Swan 114, Kingston, RI 02881, (401) 874-5931, which provides
valuable in-kind support, including graduate and undergraduate interns.

First Edition

Library of Congress Control Number: 2023951744

ISBN: 978-1-962131-01-8

THE FIRE ROAD

NICHOLAS YINGLING

BARROW STREET PRESS
NEW YORK CITY

Contents

"They're literally just feathers and bones,"
Allison Salas, a graduate student at NMSU
who has been collecting carcasses, wrote in a
Twitter thread about the die-off.

— *The Guardian*, September 2020

The Road That Breaks Fire

The road that breaks fire
we named fire.
The beach we named
for its shells, not refining

but recording the tide
that dissolves it
so close to our ears.
Forgive us for hearing

absolves. The line between
properties can burn
only so long
like a road we walk

home through the waves,
thinner and thinner.

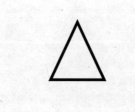

Seaside Apocalypse

All night we sleep as other people,
dreamless and on our backs. The monarchs
like an autumn of eyelids
drowse in their eucalyptus and we sip tea

and oysters at market price. We do our part.
We tip. In time the waves return
our bottles, full of yesterday's receipts.
You break even or open

says the man burning plastic and we surrender
our palms, his dogs free
to nuzzle our fortunes.
All night the scale turns. All night

the heart in fibrillation turns it back.
Yes, we say, we deserve this.

Weather in California

Tubbs Fire

I.

On the phone we talk strictly weather.
80 here. 102 in LA. How the October sun sets
midsky like a climax
shot day-for-night in some old film

where a hero must embrace his love
for six straight hours. It's a kind of romance.
Bodies rise and fall
in the deep end of a pool, the vineyard

burning, ash sinking over them
like glitter in a snow globe. Do you remember
snow on Lake Arrowhead? It hurt.
It felt nothing

like the sugar and foamite of movies,
the poppy fields of Oz
dusted with asbestos— a winter made to last
under all this light.

II.

At the Huntington maybe,
a bit *beaux-arts*-meets-Spanish-Colonial,
we were wandering

the white halls, finding Bukowski,
looking for Blake,
when we saw her: Miss Sarah Barrett

poised against the storm. (That's the sun now,
pink as her bonnet, the long ties
undone, free.)

A Lawrence painting,
she'd been paired with *The Blue Boy*,
two would-be lovers chosen

for color and century.
It tracks. The icy tones of his figure
and her small frame so full

of blood. At dusk we walked
the hedgerows, the fields of cystic cacti,
picking oranges

and roses, watching from a moon bridge
as newlyweds
ran through the falling rice.

III.

                                    There's a beat here
where the scene should end. I gut my alarm
for batteries. You smoke. Underwater
a burning house sounds muted, static
of a long-distance drag. Six hours, you say,
meaning the drive south, meaning two bodies
suspended. In 30,000 acres
of wildfire, the tagline will read, love tried
not to drown.
                                    Up to 36,000,
I say and we lose the plot in details:
the real couple in their pool, who survived,
who didn't, Miss Sarah's cough, the Tin Man's
and mine, whom the boy in blue served, how long
before
                                    the living let go.

Minimalism

You're supposed to pray
to each item, Make me happy.

Or is it, Do you make me happy?
Either way you end up the center

of an empty room. Imagine
a language with the same word

for nothing and god, the difference
being one is staged like an aria,

the other written as size:
zero-zero. When the fires came

what else was there to save?
A suit and gown in matching bags?

That calm light the fridge opens
when there's nothing left to eat?

Reading *Eat Stop Eat* under the Joshua Tree

Let the desert in. Fill yourself
and narrow
like the hourglass to the grain:
amaranth, farro, spelt.

If you must eat, eat
the ancients. If you must break
fast, break
saṃsāra and give

notice to the world: *Dear Future,*
we can go without
you. The mind
that thinks with meat

thinks it's meat.
Let your stomach do the work:
breathe. That pressure
in your chest

drops, your eyes sinking
inward like shadows on a mountain
on the clearest of days.
Don't the stars,

for all their mass, leave you
crumbs of light?
In a dream nothing can be read.
If you must

wake, wake
blank and centered as the page—
your edges so fine
you could open a finger.

Naming It

It's called dark cutting
in beef. The muscles so drained of reserves
the meat purples when exposed

to air. It's tough and unpalatable
so they grind it up.
Processing, it's called.

But there's tenderness in starving,
the body incapable of its own heat, of walking
alone with impunity. When you fell

that first time, I cradled your head
against my chest until the tremors passed.
It was so close to making love

no one would touch us.
The others stood around the patio
with their plates and drinks— how right you are

about not having friends,
we ruin their meals. Step away
from the mirror. Your stomach's only swollen.

Everything else will shrink: arms,
heart, what's between
the thighs mostly skin and hair. It's rabbit

poisoning when you take your meat
too lean, seborrhea
when there's no fat to seal the face,

your skin toweling off in the bathroom sink.
Who could call such a thing vanity?
The neighbors

phrase every want
as need. All we need
is a market just down the street, someplace

to buy coffee and vitamins
on credit. We'll call it sustainable
living or just middle-class: a life in samples,

tastes, pieces
of other people's wedding cake.

Life Here

They've been down long enough.
They've learned to see again, to pass
without bracing themselves
against the rock. What we touch, we change,
the guide says. Her flashlight moons over
the walls, still thickening
from a slow accumulation of moisture.
Life here must cling. Single cells.
Little more. They leech iron and carbon,
what seeps in
from above. The child fits. His chest
whispers through a fault
and before the main chamber— its entrance bored
into the cavern floor, a grate staircase spiraling
inwards— he's small enough
to believe in hell.
The guide must carry him on her back.
They circle down. Thirteen stories, faces
ordering out of the calcite. There will be an end,
she says. If he can hold on,
if he can just think light and trust this
stranger's body to be enough, to be the one
surface he tests his weight against, then
there will be a last step.
There, someone can claim him. By the palmprint,
the guide says, like a hand held in fire
if the hand were nothing
and the fire blown from ochre and spit.

Twelve Steps for the Holocene

The first sin was eating and so we chose
for our shape an apology. We chose

to demand less of space, to stack the fall
on our spines and pray mass

alone would be enough to hold us here.
Smoke unraveled the acacia's crown

and we tracked carbon through the snow
in endless diaspora. If the sky could touch us,

why not touch it back? If a valley could yield
to the heart's slash and burn, why not

breed new strains of hunger— colonies
of bacteria and yeast to raise us

as we raised cattle, settling stomachs,
continents, an epoch's worth of time.

What is ceremony if not the passing
from chemistry to culture. A lamb tendered

to the dawn and virgins carrying light
out of Vesta to fuel the pyres of kings,

our sooty engines, and midnight crosses,
forgiveness, convenience, we chose

the whetstone to sharpen our palates.
Fire weakened meat and meat the jaw,

our bones shifting land under glacier.
There was no walking back.

The Anorexic Dreams of Fire

Why bring back from the burning fields
a bowl full of fire and pretend that it's magic?
— Dorianne Laux

To turn away from the field
which feeds no one
twice, to feel
this too is desire

and desire must be cut
tongue by tongue
from the flame, to fill a bowl
brimming and tense

to the lip and not drink
a light that empties,
that saves
the body from being

body all the way through,
to love what leaves
a shadow
even the wind

could sweep away.

Up the Fire Road

From the Van Nuys Courthouse one is level
with the palms. Firehawks circle the valley.
The accused in his Sunday best
sits and feeds the crows.
Let it be enough for a weekday.

From the fire road one is level with the clouds.
Horses graze. A lion in a collar watches
security kick over tents
and you're the curious one
in your juror's suit, your heart rate up.

Crows gather over the helipad, the blades
of their shoulders adjusting to the downslope.
They're clever, crows.
They huddle at night in their black walnut
like gods under a wayside shrine,

remembering
each small kindness as a face.

On the Rumored Immortality of Giant Sequoia

Monarchs overwinter an evergreen
black and orange
and what can the mind do?
Rehearse fire? Measure self

against the colony, its season forever
collapsing in the wrong direction:
upwards
to some final border

that will take four generations to cross?
And the eucalyptus?
It sheds wings and is no older
than this land's conversion,

like fire, into a state. What can the mind do
but dream of shade,
an overstory that's outgrown Christ
and the Christ Father

Serra shaped from its soft heartwood.
Here. Feel where
fire opened millennia and failed.
Feel absence fall

into its own perfect column: the one
our bodies break.

On the Naming of Fire

Getty Fire

I.

Call it soft, our evacuation.

The gallery is sealing up the irises,

the sprinklers left on.

Overhead the Pacific falls

in long white veils

and out of the smoke a raven

lights upon its cypress

like a wick in reverse. It's autumn

and our maps are yellowing. Sunset.

Topanga. *The Above Place*

or just *Above*.

II.

The sisters observe simple truths. Today.
Minutes perhaps. Be present. Here this room
is for waiting, the hours for visiting
(though these too are subject to change, to fire).
Somewhere over the mountains, a white tram
carries no one backwards to a museum
I have never seen, limestone on limestone,
a geology of feather and branch—
no, be present. The Firehawks are rolling
back the water in waves. Someone's writing
a name on a sticker and pressing it
to my chest. The name is yours, comma guest.
Each year the old Colonials make way
for Mid-Century and Modern Prairie,
the white children out hunting arrowheads,
tongues of soapstone they strike like flint: nothing.
The sisters observe simple truths. The ground
beneath the ground runs deeper than family,
order, class, whatever lies in strata
so thin and hard we must pretend they're beds—
no, be present. The sisters bring fresh sheets.

III.

How will I make a little room for you in time?
Carnations and a cross. A window on subprime

châteaux; estates obscured by smoke and double pane,
the hillside cypress standing in long colonnades

a different sort of property line, growing thin
and solemn as those tinny strains of violin

that linger on the intercom. Your name, her gloves,
the nun whose throat Modigliani would have loved,

the way she wipes the ventilator clean: I've tried
to shut some details out. The body now baptized,

like chaparral, like sage or scrub or last year's fronds
in supplication to the weather we named god,

can manage fire, growth— seasons turning with the mind.
How will I make a little room for you? In time.

IV.

Topanga. *Where the summit takes the tide.*
No one's sure. Each wave
of the EKG tosses

loons on Lake Superior
one cold July
when a new husband turned first

and late in the heart
of a century you have already outlived.
Be present. A cypress burns

to a pillar of white. A raven breathes
the movement
out of stars, each feather

like a single word of day
redacted. And don't we name and rename
fire for the land

it consumes? Heat has its costs.
A stove in Duluth kept your warmth captive
on a line of gas

and the western sun
counted each nucleotide as a bead
broken from your rosary. This stranger, this guest,

he is only praying at your bedrail
to be present.
The sisters roll your body.

They read the fire map— *here*,
I was born here.

V.

It's early, for a century,
so name your savior: Christ or controlled burns,
coyotes on the switchbacks shaking ghosts from their fur
or just ash, the one material or sensory

worlds, map or matches sheltered by a palm,
the absolute or nested cypress,
the *Irises* of J. Paul Getty priceless
and fading safely under marble and alarm

or some blind graft of branches onto power lines—
whatever centers you in light.
The heart's blue meter dips, rises as a whisper might

disturb a flame.
It's here. It's gentle, just a paper sip of wine
. or peeling off a name.

Birth of an Anorexic

Not far from the cabin where you were born,
where you first learned to reach

with your soles, no bigger than wood frogs,
and feel the lining

of your mother, where they pulled you out
and taught you *kick*,

we walk through a field of dropseed
waiting for my first snow.

My fingers shrivel back into their sleeves
and you take my whole

hand in your palm, the skin loose
enough for the both of us

that I might slip in and let you deliver me
as far from winter

as your daughter did. If I asked,
you would say

I am no less of your body than hers.
You would say ash or birch,

one warmth is split from another. You let go.
Black bears are near,

their lips stripping
the branches, the last berries gelled in ice,

bunched like frogspawn.
We know them by their breath, their bellies

hot with sweetness
and beginning to cool.

The Neoliberal Neoplatonic Blues

I don't think we'll burn in the end,
not after all the polyurethane

seals our stratum and the hulls of orphaned boats
dip or rise imperceptibly.

We will walk the fire roads through fire.
I will forgive you. And you will forgive me

for measuring the sky in legroom, for believing
a stillness could hold. Even children

in their small fatigues will be welcome
to a warmth like hands

stacking up the barrel of an AR-15
to see who will go first, who will share

in that final property you'll be
embarrassed to admit is love.

I will love you. And you will love me
for the absence I trail like a bridal train

into the light. We'll enter single file, exactly
as deep as the body is wide.

That Too Is Burning Burning with What

Woolsey Fire

I.

In self there is containment.
In the concrete Buddha
sitting lotus among your aloe
there is an ammonite mistaking center
for its own. Shiva dances butoh.
A man in a surgical mask
rakes leaves. On the wrong side
of the mountain, the burned wait
to be lifted into the sky
and those who rise rise inseparable
from walls, shelves, a lifetime
of souvenirs, their horses
left to ford infinity
pools. They too will become light,
become less and less
accountable. A woman in a rosary
serves your coffee black
and on a tray four cups
of supplements. There's a crack
in that particular Siddhartha.
No one, not even the gardener,
can move him.

II.

You believe in more
         than this world
of particles and debris.
         So breathe.
You believe in parables:
         an oncologist
to the stars
         kneels, changes
auras, fire taking his
         shoulders as he might
take your coat,
         inviting you in.
You serve yourself
         tea. Gray flecks
pepper
         your turmeric
and what's scratching now
         at the back
of your throat, it feels
         so close
to ordinary
         thirst.

The Archaeopteryx Dreams of Flight

An economy hollows out the bone
and could I stop it? Could I fit
inhale into exhale and breathe air too
thin for fire or touch

this earth with only a shadow, my heart
growing and growing
faster until all that holds the chest together
is a wish, and not know

I'm trading one dimension for another?
How did it begin? As display? As a fall
so quiet and slow you could dress
the feather from the wing

and make of it currency, culture,
or some other magic.

Mulholland Love Song

With each shed
    the threat grows
louder, more musical,
    the body defined
by scales. A little
    sun draws us out
to Mulholland
    to watch the rattlers
speed their bellies
    with warm asphalt,
the slow dying
    into questions, lying
along the road
    like cast off belts.
The living must sleep
    like the dead, eyes open
under their own folds.
    They'll follow a meal
into its burrow
    until the burrow
is their own and did we
    choose to live
like this, to hold two points
    on the tongue
and still swallow
    anything?

The Savior of Mice

three percent of your daily zinc
is lost in a teaspoon
of semen tumors have a sweet tooth

and fasting can extend the life
of a mouse fifty percent

with only a small drop
in libido prayer
adds two years on average but a wife

will get you ten when you ask me
to press your carotids shut

I count to twelve
there's time for an anecdote
about the boy

who with considerable reproducibility
could Lazarus mice

using only a bowl of warm water
a timer and his hand
he had to

freeze them first— twelve
you come

to choking out *god*
dammit god dammit yes I know
the pleasures of science

of finding the miracle
rehearsed I make you smoke

in the rain seven to eleven minutes
off life expectancy at sixty
degrees a snake depresses heart

rate respiration
and if offered live prey will

ignore the rodent
its incisors heat what the snake feels
if anything we cannot say

Prism / Prescription

Begin. Even Aristotle believed
     a sparrow
wintered in the same mud
     that spawned eels
from nothing, you read
     off the optometrist's card.
Good, he says. He explains:
     the fall shifted
your sense of self— of center —
     left and one pupil
keeps pulling away, pulling
     everything
out of focus. It's tiring
     for a brain
to skip its own line,
     to force a single room
from two distinct spaces.
     You rest your eyes.
Now tell me, he says,
     where do eels come from?

Back home it's easier to live
     without detail,
our beds and the bare wall
     between us
a sort of ache. You're expanding
     in your dark.
I'm narrowing in the light
     of a screen door.
Where does she come from,
     this stranger who enters

you from the side
           when I'm not
watching? Even Bell believed
           a world, this world,
withstood being
           looked at. I close. I open
like a cell splitting into what
           I can only see
as two
           of the same cell.

Out of the Wilderness a Serpent Speaks

The eye that watches you
is not the eye

of a needle,
but a fire dilating

to its own light.
Careful, my friend.

You can eat a literal hole
in that heart.

The Neoliberal Pastoral Blues

The burro takes a carrot from your hand.
In her coat seeds of field and fire
twist themselves so deep
the stablehand must cut them out.

Like anything with a history
the land requires maintenance and he thins
the chaparral, doubling
La Raza with a voice somehow truer

for singing just
beyond your understanding. Forgive him
if he first took you for a priest.
It's the suit. It's slimming

and what could be nobler these days, to live
full as cheatgrass in such a climate?
The burro takes another carrot.
Each bite makes a tiny crack

of thunder. *Lluvia*, the stablehand says.
Lluvia, you say.
He gestures with his palm
and what might the priest offer him? A carrot?

A name? Your name? It meant young man
centuries ago.

I Take Shelter under the Stables

because it's hailing in the desert
and the horses seem unmoved
by a sky full of loose teeth. The mare
alone starts and though her bite
could unstring a hand, mine reaches.
As a child I chewed the world
into self and not self. *Blanket. Grass.*
The mare too has grown by division—
cells splitting, muscles tearing
and mending, her heart that could burst
through this gate, five full pumps
a second, slowing now, locking
stride with my touch. *Muzzle. Mane.*
My fingers trace between the eyes.
Here. Here my two halves meet
the thin blade of her blindness.
The hail stops. In the rain I am what?
A single organ of sense? I see
rust on the bars, poppies on the hill,
and in another country painted ladies
hang their patterned wings to dry.

Autophagy: A Triptych

All winter life fed

      on itself, the ground full

of rattlesnakes, and now the rattlesnakes

      full of ground

squirrel grow back

      their heartmeat, their spring

muscle and fat. Each cell

      in the earth's stillness flagged

last year's proteins

      like a logger tagging trunks with paint

and so the body recycles

      its own age— starvation

for the cure, LA's

dream of lasting youth.
Adults powerwalk the canyon.

Their children uncouple
the ouroboros into two rattlers. Each

step up the fire road makes me pure
metabolism, makes me lighter

on this earth. I stop to rest beneath
a live oak. Perhaps its shadow

swallows mine. Perhaps
they meet and blur like lovers

out of film's golden age.
When my grandfather died

that first time he faded
in on a technicolor meadow.

Flesh, he said, is not the actor
but the screen. It's a god-

eat-god world and the best lose

all appetite. I watch you
measure each meal
by the size of a fist (your doctor's

orders). On the wall
we've hung two carpenters—
Karen and Christ,

patron saints of the anonymous
purgers and restrictors
who ask to be filled

by a higher power.
About half will
relapse. Each month

you get a new chip to remind you
recovery's still a coin toss.
Our quinoa boils.

Rings of germ appear,
these little halos of sun and starch
that sustain us

we call tails.

On the Interstate

You may drive through the dawn
to find just another grass fire

in the night we are putting out.
If you imagine another side

do you imagine a wall between?
Some passage wide enough

for a pollinator? Or do they hang
there like flyers for the missing?

What bothers you more?
An unmarked grave or monarchs

made to petal it? A hand feeding
the soft flames of an ocotillo

or the ocotillo like so many hands
made to open?

The Anorexics Dream of Flight

I.

Imagine years of famine as a map
folded into our mothers' chromosomes:
a migration, a longing to winter

somewhere over the gulf. To better fly
songbirds gave up sweetness.
Imagine survival with only a taste

of milkweed in our prey: bitter, acrid
as all that wild brushland burning upwind.
Imagine the horizon as hunger.

Imagine the tongue as phantom pain.
Would we sing?

II.

Tomorrow we'll leave this city.
      We'll order the driest, whitest wines
by the flight and fill out
      the papers. Will you? I do.
And so on. And if the 405 is stopped dead by ten
      thousand painted ladies touching
our windshield—
      each a small blessing of oil— we'll take the 101.
Let the dying fill our vision
      with gold. To open wide
in full color,

a painted lady must digest itself first,
      heart, brain, and all.
I've heard it called a soup,
      my marrow. Soup, cigarettes, black coffee,
and speed lifted Dorothy
      forever out of Kansas and tomorrow
we'll click our heels and say, Let it
      burn, and never speak of calories. Or both.
It's okay, Love, to want both
      of everything. Two wings. Too much. To know
the fallout

in honey, the plastic
      in placenta, and still eat forever
chemicals straight from the blood stream. And if fire
      smokes the resin right
out of teeth, we'll shotgun the neighbors
      into our folds. All stomach

and cortex, all marbled
         with gray matter, we'll see clearly for miles
and that aching blur between
         your eyes will heal at last
into four years of my letters, which all begin the same:

III.

Dear Sierra,
Don't be afraid to stand.

There's so much atmosphere
in your name.
And you can always drop
it and be the middle Rose

who loves our rich
earth for cleaning us like a child
cleans their plate. And the child?
We'll name them something grounded, something

rooted like Hope. To better fly
songbirds gave up
sweetness. Love, imagine
a whole second act just walking home.

Picture it: an empty highway, wild poppies
nursing our ladies to sleep,
the whole era of exhaust
passing slowly from our brainstems,

maybe an apple stand with two slices of pie.
We won't have to share
anything.
The pavement so full of lanes,

could we ever really cross
together?

Magical Thinking

The life before cement is ghosting up
— Eloise Klein Healy

0. Eclipse

We've tucked the skylights in, stapled the curtains
to the wall. Still the night won't close,
not completely. In a pale orbit of your hair I sit

watching the sky as if what it does it does so
with purpose, like these dusky string lights
that pass for the souls of orange groves

drawn back to Los Angeles by the August heat.
I turn them off. You're inside, spinning the walls.
When you struck the cement

like a match, some light went out for good
and now I must hold you through each eclipse,
each passing shadow of that other world— the one

where I caught you or your last lover hadn't
sunk craters in the drywall the size of your head.
No one meant to hurt you forever,

not when you asked if you looked like Jean Seberg
and I said, Yes, as Joan of Arc, or when you said,
Tell me the truth, and I told you

how the moon returns from being impossibly thin,
how gravity clings to our missing pieces
and one day they will close a lid on the sun

and kings, priests, soldiers will tremble and pray.

I. When the Temperature Finally Drops

under a hundred, we feed carrots
to the horses. The sorrel cools herself
in dirt while a groom kneels, ready
to measure her chest to withers— the heart
girth, how we determine weight.

From the stables I watch you
steady yourself against a eucalyptus.
Last time we blamed electrolytes
and sugar. We blamed stress and heat.
But when the scale settled

on two digits, I couldn't help
but count the plates stacked neatly
in your spine, in your hands
that shallow bowl of bloat you try
but cannot empty. I see you haven't

lost your balance at all. You're stripping
the blue gum, your hands peeling
bark like a sunburn, like skin
off an onion. Beneath the shedding
she's smooth as marble. Her trunk splits

its two perfect limbs and we can't help
but touch. Daphne with the sun
at her heel, why reach for clouds
when you could dive deep into this earth?

II. The Prelapsarian Blues

She takes shears to her waistline and breathes
freely. He is deciding where to sit,

a pond where koi shape their murk like hands
at the potter's wheel or a flat stone

laid beneath the eucalyptus: YOU ARE HERE.
She is leaving soon for the valley below,

its bodies that work, another Idle Hour's
burlesque. The law of dependent origination

permits them little choice. She picks an apricot
with open sores, some other mouth

having only made it sweeter. He sits.
He meditates on the straightness of his spine,

on a man left alone, undressing for the garden
mirror— that curious arc of his own sex

reversed. He doesn't touch. He counts each breath,
each rib by the shade that grows between.

III. Medusa

after Aimee Nezhukumatathil

You choose the one-piece with frills.
The child's swimsuit you think
will hide your stomach,
that medusa you eye through the mirror
and suck in. After years
of floating by on stimulants,
you're trying out weight. It's a lot
to balance and at the beach you ask again
if you look three-years old
or six-months pregnant. Your breasts
in the water shallow and pink
as moon jellies. When starved
certain species can eat their own bell,
shrink back into a polyp,
begin again. What you're asking is
which would be worse?
Lighter now, you let the tide carry you
farther out, into an immensity
that scares me. Love, the Pacific is full
of sea nettles. Their cups
pour a fire older than pain or blood,
golden as the eggs that drift
on your wide current. So fine and thin,
so close to water,
they disappear on dry land.

IV. A Knowledge of Fruit

In Los Angeles everyone needs therapy.
I prefer the chanting of monks
streaming at 432Hz as I lie on this mattress
in an otherwise empty room.
The most strictly anorexic anorexic
in program, you say, is a nun.
What is it that you want to know?
My father washed his hands after every meal
and my mother paid me to help
with her garden. I remember her fingers
weaving deep into a cut honeydew.
The flies, spoil, and sweat. The rodents
running bloated through the yard.
Yes, we'd shower after,
me hiding between her legs, my face red
with pomegranate gore. And her scar?
In Los Angeles this all means something
about you, twisting the cotton tail
of your tampon, or the brothers
I never had or how your blood tastes
metallic against my tongue like a penny
too corroded for a face, how you wipe mine
clean, my head held to your stomach
as a child holds a gourd,
how it splits at his feet into any,
into every phase of the moon but full.

V. The Limits of Magic

When the boy grew bored with summer
Grandmother fetched stones from the river.
She said, You will be a hare,
and with her brush showed him how
a few lines can soften granite into fur.
He began to believe then in small touches.
He painted snappers and box turtles,
returning them to the Yuba
where they could cast a spell over minnows
or any child brave enough to risk a toe.

At thirty-five, he weighs her boxes down
with old hares. Varnish wears thin,
then color, then children
sift the backwaters for gold
and pyrite and copper-bellied newts.
No one's told them. There's no part of the newt
it can't regrow, an eye, a limb, a heart.
They know only that the newt is quick.
Its skin mixing deeper shades of sleep,
the riverbed is blank enough and moves.

VI. Clay Bodies

out of earth: not Adam but a lip
smoothed around emptiness   and held
to our own: what's thrown upon the wheel feels
uniform but is composed

of sediment: iron buff silica and so we too
shadow smoke   its crude mass of terracotta rising
over the valley: carbon
monoxide dioxide soot: we watch for form

what shape will come   between the inside and outside
of burning: a hand steady   as a servant
carries porcelain or a priest
his vessel or the mother   her child:

its head soft but closing:
out of the bell   the belly of an urn

VII: The Buddha Dreams of Milk and Permanence

In eating, you
forget you too

are the source. Life,
little more

than a fluke, than a thousand
segments of tape

worm, takes hold
with no need

of its own
intestine, mouth, or these

buds of tissue
my rebirth keeps

hardening: teeth
to push the teeth

through.

VIII. The Postlapsarian Blues

You're naked
on a digital scale. I'm naked
at the window, knowing whatever is

outside sees us
as we are: clouds and power
lines, this scrub jay trying to enter

the jay that is already here,
already part of the surface my hand
presses against.

This bird in the man
in the glass: had I imagined
some other side

of self, one that would or could break
first? You touch my arm.
You remind me that you fell too—

a brief spasm and then
unconsciousness. Be with me,
you say, here, now. Like a vanity

the present folds
around us: in one you're using two
fingers to coax what's left of me

out of yourself and in another
you're slipping half
a wishbone under urine.

In the third, a man,
inversed, is making you
feel so small. He says, What passes

through us we can only hope
to stain, like the scrub jay,
like the mother

in a cathedral
window: blue.

IX. The Tao of Refeeding

It takes a patient
body, each number
spinning
through the *I*

of the scale.
Where it lands
you are still. Everything
else turns

like a stomach,
an emptiness
somehow aware
of all it is

missing—
a hunger.

X. Love, We Never Get Too Far

from water. We can walk this fire
road down to the Pacific
and hear waves break once
into two directions. We're soft.
We're the final shape, our hands
bridging shores on the canyon wall
or at least holding us
up. In their stillness mollusks,
like ossicles, tell us where we stand.

from the fall. I pray with lips
pressed to the fault line,
each drink weeping slowly
out the back of your head. Exhaust. Dust.
You settle into lateness, a post-
concussive. Like a ghost, you say.
Like the soul it never quite shows up
on an MRI, but here you are,
just out of focus or faith.

from bottom. The shallow end
lets you watch your step.
Drowning, you know,
is as much a predicament of time
as water. You backstroke.
You open turn, the surface snapping
against the concrete as real
as anything left
unsaid— a feeling, a love, a song

of whales held in our mountain
like a breath.

XI. Step Work (Against Extinction)

Even the pool winces at rain.
Focus, you remember,
is Latin for hearth. Have you
resisted the temperature of a room

or like the sun have you sustained others
by consuming yourself
cold? Who taught you to nourish cold,
to starve this low-grade fever

the world calls self? *He broke it,*
saying, This is my body,
which is for you. Know that
you want it. You do,

no matter how much
you cry when we feed it to you.

XII. Notes from the Underground

The new gods
        are not the pullers of strings
but the strings themselves, down in the soil
        recomposing matter
into moon lace. The dead are fine,
        your doctor says. Those you lost in the fall
are calm, but the living
        neurons that have grown
dependent, that keep firing
        into absence, they create a kind of noise,
a grief.

Heads of *cubensis*
        snap in two, each a wafer
with gills. Between the shore and dawn
        we interstate.
We disappear into sequoia. Eyes closed, listening
        for what fingers below
play the world's green music, I offer you
        my hand. Slowly
the signals in your head quiet,
        let go. There's a trail here
worn between the upper and lower branches,

a space made for
        or by
something like us.

On the Rumored Immortality of the Cloud

Some change in light may be necessary.
Each wave forms. Each platelet
passes through the heart like a cloud
passes through our pool and still we wake
in need of an ocean.
Yes, we can leave early.

                                                We're in control
of the wheel, that after-hours feeling
in my hand like any network
signing off, like snow falling
on abandoned malls or the interstate
we will leave this world still
pointing a way home.

                                         Yes, we can stay.
We have the light and a tide to endure
its own long becoming, its drift
glass soft under our feet
and softer for the time each wave takes—
an ocean, a hand, always
the taking

                                         that repeats itself.

Things You Wouldn't Believe

We did our best. We got used to the taste.
Apricots spoiled the yard and we pressed coffee
and practiced being all morning.
Be still, we said and to the animals

we gave a dead language for names,
never guessing the end would come so
nostalgic for a carousel,
the white child riding a white horse and the bay

sepia as a souvenir photograph. Be empty, we said
and ate an ocean out of taffy, the pavement
out of Pall Malls, and from the ferry
we watched for life in our wake— blooms

of *chrysaora* and latex. We were young.
Most nights a hand found its way
to breastbone or the small of a back.
There was forgiveness. There was forgiveness

and it was ours to give.

Introduction to the Sacred

Camp Fire

clarity comes after fire—
the cobwebs made visible   those small galaxies

of hunger and ash   you've learned to live without
power   you've cleared the horseshoes

from your land   the keys a neighbor's
steel hip   what some call luck

just the weight of movement   holding us here
people ask   what's the last thing you remember

of Paradise   and you tell them
the sky ripened its one navel orange   or it rained

primary colors   your windshield melting
but it was a woman   naked in the pines nursing

the cut   stem of her catheter and what was running out
you tried to stop

Containment

The blood of the rich is full tonight
of strange furniture.
It's getting harder to read,

our eyes thinning like an atmosphere.
At night our other senses rally

at the borders of sight. A hand reaches
for some boundary,
the line of a body and the surrounding dark

locked together like a zipper's teeth.
We wake between two horizons.

Malibu burns. We fold a red moon
in the linens
as a woman in a respirator might

lead three horses through the canyon,
knowing her trailer can only hold two,

knowing one light rises
to meet the other.

From the Trial of Joan of Arc

When the moon is much older
than you think
and the trees die soft and tomorrow

lifts from its nest of gravity
so you might break it with your hands,

finding no stars
as you have broken vows
and found only the emptiness between

rain, come to me.
Come to me when fires

drink down the night
in vain and the body is a dry fountain
burning itself out,

no one left to care
for the bones beneath your worship

and the river filling with children
who breathe
chrome from paper bags,

when your intentions, like mountains,
grow hazy by midday

in this, our city of boundaries.
Come when exhaust sleeps
in the laurel and these arms in their restraints

curl out like a candelabrum,
each IV hole black

as a wick burnt down. Softly
you may blow into them:
small prayers against darkness.

Last Night's Construction

paper confettis the pool, this one black sheet
like a door left open in water. I apologize.
Lighters appear like manna from heaven.
Heaven appears a sky hungover

with gunpowder and glitter. I reach in
and ladle a monarch. Milkweed. Tiger. Blackvein.
In my palm the slow curtsy of wings
makes faith seem like something I could take

apart with my hands, something I could hide
among the ashtrays and origami.
Isn't this the desert, the city for drying out?
It folds and fans. It rests. A sunset

stained on glass or a child's
watercolor flooded with design, it has a chance.

On the Rumored Immortality of Art

For depth he substitutes layers:
the Atlantic all sundown and ice floe,
a few black and white
auks left unfinished in the dusk.

This is *trompe l'oeil*, of course. The birds
long dead, the painter
will be forced to buy one in town
already posed. He shoulders his flintlock

over the current, his boots
haloed by the dying
hour and the ripples opening wider and wider
until he too is *pentimento*

and somewhere waves of another sea
wash onto the same continent,
warmer and warmer
in color— an impression of morning

blazing over the mountains.
It's a touch Romantic for our artist:
all that wild brush and one giant sequoia
to draw the eye,

to take each burning ring in, year after year,
and keep growing.

Down from the Fire Road

for Kari

It's early enough to see the mountains.
Jetstreams unravel to sky. A red-tail
converts a diamondback into distance, warmth—
and it's gone, your word for such an image.
Undeserved? How we came to it together
from different sides like the coyote
who passes me on the street, treading up
as I tread down. Light here takes a hard line
between cypress and her coat fills with shade
and empties and fills again with ease,
a branch of what is ash in name only.
I know it's late but I offer you this
small concession: yes, all there is is life
and it's early enough to see the mountains.

Against Life Expectancy

Today I read that it's an act of faith
to plant trees in California, that this oak
whose shade eases the fire road
has a slimmer chance of surviving
the coming decade than me. And here I am
pushing acorns into the dirt. Each day
I rise and nourish this body with more
than a cup of rice or tea. Softness fills in
like a gray moss between my joints
and the muscles stretch to stand
without fear of falling. I offer my shadow
to the live oak and in return morning
offers itself to me as change singing light
from the bottom of a fountain.
Out of acorns, I plant a copper cent
between the roots. 1986. A wish
that can no longer afford to feed me.
Whatever I am, I am not such small tender.
I've grown. Like this oak, I've grown
toward two hungers and could live
no other way.

The Wild Kindness

All night we sleep as other people,
heavy, the tide beneath us
like a stranger's bed
we leave unmade. In time the waves return

our city, or at least the pieces we failed
to breathe. We make small talk
over breakfast about phytoplankton
feeding off the ash

or how the yellow eel silvers itself,
its stomach dissolving
to make way for that final organ
as if love were some end to nourishment,

something cold and dreamless in our bodies
cutting through the current,
choosing for us
the one way we will empty ourselves.

In the distance two dogs shake
off the surf. They roll.
They chew through the new flesh
of their burns, knowing deep in their cells

somehow
the gold will grow back.

Scale and Feather

No one dies, dear reader,
not in this poem. And I hope,
though there is much talk in poetry
about the art of unknowing,
no one dies in the next either.
Until then best to concern ourselves
with smaller questions:
what a half bottle of wine has to do
with the wind or forgiveness
with these shadows of *lepidoptera*
blotting out Los Angeles.
Try to ignore for a minute
any arrhythmia like a day-moon
in your chest and I'll try to remember
my 3.3 almost passes
for a white blood cell count.
There's a cost for looking inward.
Lepidoptera makes a wing of scales
or scale of wings. I'm not sure
but sometimes the heron flies,
all feather and joint, and the koi
are fine. The day balances
like a mug on your knee. Yes,
you planted the wrong milkweed
last year, whatever that means.
Still the monarchs came.

No Outlet

Everywhere in America there are caution signs.
Firehawks circle the valley. The hills asleep
look middle aged
and just as dangerous. Soon, the billboard reads.

Outside a child in a yellow slicker crosses
a star chart of yellowed leaves
as if to say:
how gentle, this collision of heaven and earth.

Over coffee and eggs our lips spill a rich syllable.
Thoughts drift from us like pollen
on a river
whose end we'll never see. It's Sunday now

and there's no paper. The roads are closed.
The water is rising.

Sit with me.

Acknowledgments

My thanks to the editors of the following magazines in which versions of these poems previously appeared, sometimes under different names:

32 Poems: "Things You Wouldn't Believe"; *The Adroit Journal*: "Reading *Eat Stop Eat* Under The Joshua Tree"; *Bellevue Literary Review*: "Magical Thinking: Love, We Never Get Too Far"; *Bellingham Review*: "Birth of An Anorexic" and "From The Trial of Joan of Arc"; *Best New Poets*: "The Anorexics Dream of Flight"; *Cherry Tree*: "Twelve Steps for The Holocene"; *Colorado Review*: "Magical Thinking: When the Temperature Finally Drops"; *Crab Creek Review*: "The Anorexic Dreams of Fire" and "Introduction to the Sacred"; *Diode*: "Down from the Fire Road" and "Prism / Prescription"; *EcoTheo Review*: "Autophagy: A Triptych"; *Fourteen Hills*: "Magical Thinking: A Knowledge of Fruit"; *Frontier*: "Magical Thinking: Eclipse"; *Good River Review*: "The Archaeopteryx Dreams of Flight"; *Grist*: "Magical Thinking: Medusa"; *The Idaho Review*: "The Road That Breaks Fire"; *Lake Effect*: "Against Life Expectancy"; *The Missouri Review*: "On the Rumored Immortality of The Cloud," "Up the Fire Road," and "Weather in California"; *Moon City Review*: "Seaside Apocalypse" and "The Wild Kindness"; *Nimrod*: "Magical Thinking: the Limits of Magic"; *Notre Dame Review*: "Life Here" and "Naming It"; *Ocean State Review*: "Minimalism"; *The Penn Review*: "Scale and Feather"; *Pleiades*: "On The Naming of Fire"; *Ruminate*: "Magical Thinking: Clay Bodies"; *Slipstream*: "That Too is Burning Burning with What"; *Spillway*: "No Outlet"; *Star 82 Review*: "Containment"; *Sugar House Review*: "Mulholland Love Song"; *Tupelo Quarterly*: "I Take Shelter Under the Stables"; *Whale Road Review*: "On the Rumored Immortality of Art" and "On the Rumored Immortality of Giant Sequoia."

"On the Naming of Fire" was reprinted in *Poetry Daily* (as "The Cypress King").

Deepest gratitude to Shannon, Peter, and everyone at Barrow Street for their time and support. And a special thank you to Rachel Rothenberg for her dedication, patience, and insight, for the care she showed this work. These poems owe her.

Thank you to my teachers, particularly Katie, Joe, and Judy. Dylan, Bill, anyone who ever read a draft, thank you. Kari Flickinger, who saved me from prose, I wish you were here to read this.

Love to my parents for years of unwavering encouragement.

And Sierra, of course, for being there before and after all the poems, in the flesh.

NICHOLAS YINGLING is a writer, educator, and caregiver. His poems have appeared widely, including in *Poetry Daily*, *The Adroit Journal*, *Nimrod*, *Pleiades*, and *Colorado Review*. He holds degrees from UC Berkeley and UC Davis and currently lives in Los Angeles.

BARROW STREET POETRY

Brother Nervosa
Ronald Palmer 2024

The Fire Road
Nicholas Yingling 2024

Fanling in October
Pui Ying Wong 2023

Close Red Water
Emma Aylor 2023

Landscape with Missing River
Joni Wallace 2023

Down Low and Lowdown...
Timothy Liu 2023

*the archive is all
in present tense*
Elizabeth Hoover 2022

Person, Perceived Girl
A.A. Vincent 2022

Frank Dark
Stephen Massimilla 2022

Liar
Jessica Cuello 2021

*On the Verge of
Something Bright and Good*
Derek Pollard 2021

*The Little Book of
No Consolation*
Becka Mara McKay 2021

Shoreditch
Miguel Murphy 2021

Hey Y'all Watch This
Chris Hayes 2020

Uses of My Body
Simone Savannah 2020

Vortex Street
Page Hill Starzinger 2020

*Exorcism Lessons
in the Heartland*
Cara Dees 2019

American Selfie
Curtis Bauer 2019

Hold Sway
Sally Ball 2019

Green Target
Tina Barr 2018

*Luminous Debris: New &
Selected Legerdemain*
Timothy Liu 2018

*We Step into the Sea: New
and Selected Poems*
Claudia Keelan 2018

Adorable Airport
Jacqueline Lyons 2018

Whiskey, X-ray, Yankee
Dara-Lyn Shrager 2018

For the Fire from the Straw
Heidi Lynn Nilsson 2017

Alma Almanac
Sarah Ann Winn 2017

A Dangling House
Maeve Kinkead 2017

Noon until Night
Richard Hoffman 2017

Kingdom Come Radio Show
Joni Wallace 2016

In Which I Play the Run Away
Rochelle Hurt 2016

*The Dear Remote
Nearness of You*
Danielle Legros Georges 2016

Detainee
Miguel Murphy 2016

*Our Emotions Get Carried Away
Beyond Us*
Danielle Cadena Deulen 2015

Radioland
Lesley Wheeler 2015

Tributary
Kevin McLellan 2015

Horse Medicine
Doug Anderson 2015

This Version of Earth
Soraya Shalforoosh 2014

Unions
Alfred Corn 2014

O, Heart
Claudia Keelan 2014

Last Psalm at Sea Level
Meg Day 2014